Romanticism
By Jessica Gunderson
Movements in Art Series
Continuing Series of 8 with 4 New Titles
978-1-58341-613-6
$32.80 (List) $22.95 (Net) each
48 pages
Reading Level: Grades 5 and up
Color and historical photographs and artwork
Release date: Fall 2008
LOC 2007008495

An examination of the art movement known as
Romanticism from its beginnings in the late 1700s to its
decline in the mid-1800s, including an introduction to
great artists and works—such as the Arc de Triomphe in
Paris and Spanish artist Francisco de Goya.

Contact Info:
Lona Maker
Creative Education—An Imprint of
The Creative Company
PO Box 227
Mankato, MN 56002
507.388.9207
lmaker@thecreativecompany.us

Movements in Art ROMANTICISM

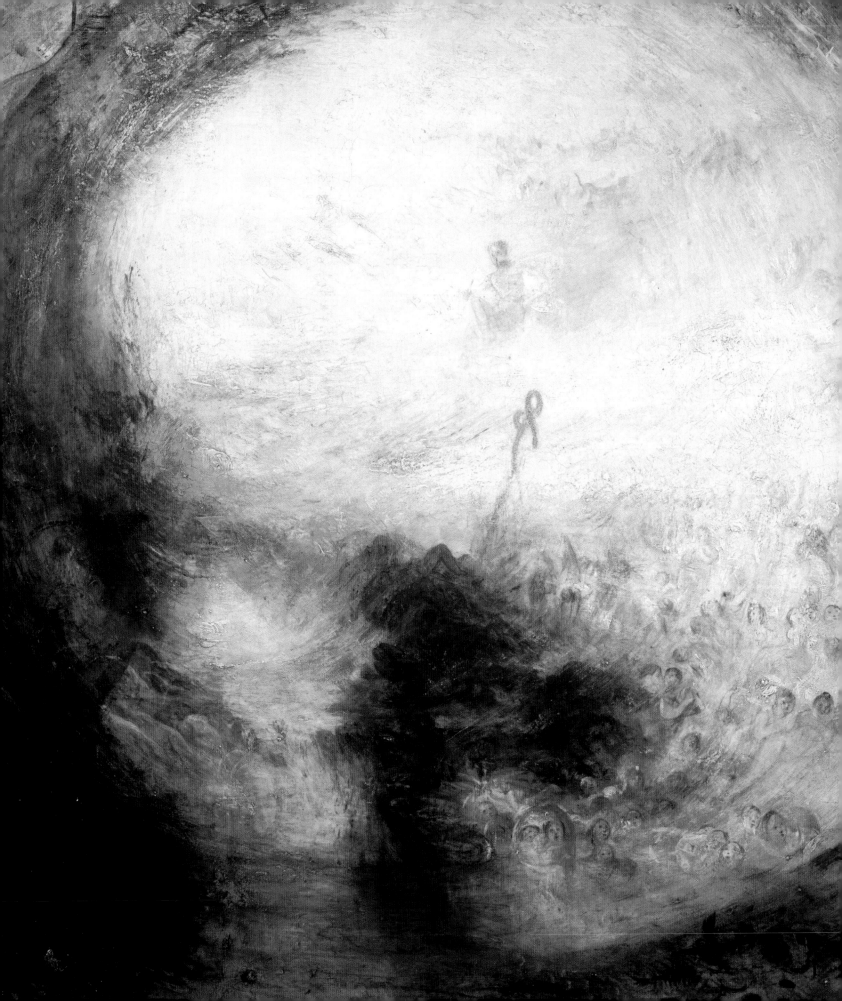

Movements in Art **ROMANTICISM**

JESSICA GUNDERSON

CREATIVE EDUCATION

Published by Creative Education
P.O. Box 227, Mankato, Minnesota 56002
Creative Education is an imprint of The Creative Company.

Design and production by Blue Design (www.bluedes.com)
Art direction by Rita Marshall
Printed in the United States of America

Photographs by Alamy (Bildarchiv Monheim GmbH, Mary Evans Picture
Library, The Print Collector, SC Photos, Visual Arts Library (London)), The
Bridgeman Art Library (Henry Fuseli, Nicolas Henri Jeaurat de Bertry), Cor-
bis (Gustave Moreau, Steven Vidler/Eurasia Press), Getty Images (William
Blake, Etienne Carjat, John Constable, Eugène Delacroix, French School,
Caspar David Friedrich, Alexander Gardner//Time Life Pictures, Joe Griffin/
Hulton Archive, Baron Antoine Jean Gros, Hulton Archive, Imagno, Imagno/
Austrian Archives, Kean Collection, ND/Roger Viollet, Odilon Redon, Lau-
rent Victor Rose, Francois Rude, Tate Gallery)

Library of Congress Cataloging-in-Publication Data

Gunderson, Jessica.
Romanticism / by Jessica Gunderson.
p. cm. — (Movements in art)
Includes index.
ISBN 978-1-58341-613-6
1. Romanticism in art—Juvenile literature. I. Title. II. Series.

N6465.R6G86 2008
709.03'42—dc22   2007008495

First edition

9 8 7 6 5 4 3 2 1

Cover: **Dante and Virgil in the Underworld** *by Eugène Delacroix (1822)*
Page 2: **Light and Color (Goethe's Theory)—The Morning after the Deluge**
 by J. M. W. Turner (1843)
Pages 4–5: **Women of Algiers in Their Apartment** *by Eugène Delacroix (1834)*

Romanticism

The history of the world can be told through accounts of great battles, the lives of kings and queens, and the discoveries and inventions of scientists and explorers. But the history of the way people think and feel about themselves and the world is told through art. From paintings of the hunt in prehistoric caves, to sacred art in the Middle Ages, to the abstract forms of the 20th century, movements in art are the expression of a culture. Sometimes that expression is so powerful and compelling that it reaches through time to carry its message to another generation.

From the sublime landscapes (opposite) of German painter Caspar David Friedrich to the passionate insights into humanity made by Frenchman Théodore Géricault (above), the emotionally charged Romantic movement changed the history of art.

Friedrich's *Wanderer above the Sea of Fog* (1818) exemplifies the Romantic sensibility that one's perception of art—and of the world—depends upon having a private, intimate relationship with nature and a desire to know oneself fully.

With its ghosts and dreams, heroes and villains, **epic** landscapes and stormy skies, Romantic art turned the tide of tradition. The Romantic era stretched from 1750 to 1850, a time of political and social upheaval in Western Europe. Before this time, reason had been the basis on which to evaluate art, but Romantic artists challenged this idea with their focus on internal passions and the human **subconscious**, bringing to the surface the age-old debate of reason versus emotion. The Romantic spirit pushed the boundaries of tradition and gave art a fresh dose of passion and freedom that is still potent today.

THE AGE OF ENLIGHTENMENT

In the 18th century, political and social changes were sweeping across Europe and North America. The scientific discoveries of previous centuries, including the fact that Earth revolved around the sun, led many to question their religious beliefs. New methods of transportation gave people in rural areas access to education, and as members of the middle class became more educated, they grew unhappy with being ruled by the church or the **monarchy**. In France, armed revolutionaries overthrew the monarchy and replaced it with a new government. In colonial America, settlers rebelled against British rule.

Philosophers such as English-American Thomas Paine, John Locke of England, and Jean-Jacques Rousseau of Switzerland had a great impact on the changes that were occurring. They believed that scientific thought and reason were essential to an effective government and that systematic thinking could be applied to all forms of human activities and ways of life, not just to science and research. Common people soaked up these ideas with enthusiasm. As members of the middle class became more educated, they gained power by holding positions in the government and the field of science. This era of new thoughts and ideas became known as the Age of Enlightenment, or the Age of Reason.

The value of scientific inquiry filtered into literature, music, painting, and sculpture. Artistic tendencies shifted toward restraint and **formality**. Painters, sculptors, and architects looked toward Classical Greek and Roman works as their models, and history was increasingly valued as subject matter. A new movement, called Neoclassicism, had begun.

Although Neoclassicism was the dominant art style of the early 18th century, a separate movement was also taking shape. Many artists were moving away from the sober Neoclassical style toward a more uninhibited and emotional style called Romanticism. During this time, the word "romance" did not mean love. Rather, it referred to tales written in the Romance languages (languages derived from Latin, such as French, Spanish, and Italian). Often, these tales were **medieval** in setting, highly imaginative, and fantastical.

Romantic artists rebelled against the rules and constraints of Neoclassicism. Just as revolutions would tear down old governments, Romantic artists believed in tearing down old ideas and traditions. They did not believe that

COMMON SENSE;

ADDRESSED TO THE

INHABITANTS

OF

AMERICA,

On the following interesting

SUBJECTS.

I. Of the Origin and Design of Government in general, with concise Remarks on the English Constitution.

II. Of Monarchy and Hereditary Succession.

III. Thoughts on the present State of American Affairs.

IV. Of the present Ability of America, with some miscellaneous Reflections.

Man knows no Master save creating HEAVEN,
Or those whom choice and common good ordain.
THOMSON.

PHILADELPHIA;

Printed, and Sold, by R. BELL, in Third-Street,
MDCCLXXVI.

Thomas Paine's pamphlet, *Common Sense*, was one of the first publications made available to American colonists that presented the arguments in favor of American independence in language that was accessible to the common person.

Antoine-Jean Gros admired Napoleon Bonaparte and painted the future emperor's likeness many times, using his characteristically fluid lines and delicate coloration. Here, a determined Napoleon is pictured leading his army in November 1796, about eight months after having been appointed commander in chief of the Army of Italy.

humanity could be governed by a strict set of rules or understood by systematic formulas. Instead, the Romantics felt that humans were propelled by more indefinable concepts such as love, greed, and fear. Emotion, not reason, was the basis for their new artistic style. While Neoclassical art was calm, restrained, and clear, Romantic art was imaginative, dreamlike, dramatic, and filled with emotional intensity.

In France, the turbulent years of the French Revolution (1789–99) had a profound impact on art. With the fall of the monarchy in 1792, the people of France gained a new sense of individuality. No longer did they feel bound to the societal class they had been born into, be it royalty or working class. Self-determination—the idea that one is in control of one's own destiny— became a foundation for society. With this new focus on individuality and the importance of the mind, many French artists felt freed from the old constraints of society. Their ambition now was to construct a new world from the remnants of the old. No longer did they have to produce art to please royalty or the wealthy; now they could express their own ideas and imaginations through their work. Heroes of the past were resurrected in new, more imaginative ways, and heroes of the present were not given Classical lines and poses, but were portrayed as almost supernatural beings wrought with emotion and grandeur.

One of the first French Romantic painters was an artist named Antoine-Jean Gros (1771–1835), a passionate young man who rebelled against the seriousness of Neoclassicism. Gros was drawn to the more emotional aspects of painting, such as the use of vibrant, rich colors and sweeping brushstrokes. He was also enthralled with the magic of the battlefield. Like his master,

THE FRENCH REVOLUTION

On July 14, 1789, a mob of angry civilians stormed the Bastille prison in Paris in pursuit of arms and ammunition, setting off the French Revolution. For years, the French people had been poor and hungry, but King Louis XVI and Queen Marie-Antoinette had done nothing to help their situation. The king and his wife were later jailed, and in 1793, they were tried for treason and beheaded. A political party known as the Jacobins rose to power and put into place a government that was radical and unstable. The Jacobins were responsible for mass executions throughout France, and their reign became known as the Reign of Terror. In 1799, Napoleon Bonaparte overthrew the remaining Jacobins in power and declared himself emperor of France.

In *Napoleon in the Plague House at Jaffa*, Gros displays how there was nothing the ambitious young general believed he could not do in 1799—including healing people stricken by the plague. Months later, Napoleon took over the French government.

NAPOLEON BONAPARTE

Napoleon Bonaparte was a military general who helped defend France from invading armies, such as the Prussians and Austrians, during the French Revolution. In 1799, in the midst of political struggle in France, he declared himself dictator of the country. He ruled France for 15 years, and in that time, his army invaded several countries and established the vast Na-

poleonic Empire, which encompassed most of western Europe. Napoleon was obsessed with power and image, and he employed several artists, including Jean-Antoine Gros, to glorify him into a myth on canvas. Artists in other countries also depicted Napoleon, though in less flattering ways. In Spain, Francisco de Goya commemorated the Spanish resistance against Napoleon, and British artist J. M. W. Turner painted an image of Napoleon in exile.

Neoclassical painter Jacques-Louis David (1748–1825), he was **commissioned** by Napoleon Bonaparte, who took over the French government in 1799, to paint war scenes, but unlike David, who depicted them realistically, Gros portrayed the scenes with a focus on emotion and unreality. His painting *Napoleon in the Plague House at Jaffa* (1804) has many mystical tendencies, including a red sky, the exotic locale of North Africa, and haunting images of the dying, whom Napoleon is shown healing with a near-godlike ability. Later in life, Gros turned to Neoclassical painting, but he had a strong influence on the following generations of Romantic artists.

In Great Britain in the late 18th and early 19th centuries, Romantic literature prevailed. English poets such as Lord Byron and Percy Bysshe Shelley used nature as their inspiration. They wrote of nature being wild and without logic, and their poems evoked strong feelings in their readers. In both literature and **ethics**, emotion became more important than reason. This attitude filtered to British landscape painters, who saw nature not as rational and scientific, but as eerie, thrilling, and terrifying. They believed that the closer one got to nature, the closer one would be to the truth of the world. As did Romantic poetry, Romantic paintings depicted nature as filled with melancholy, loneliness, and loss.

Artists of the Romantic period aimed for the **sublime** as opposed to the **picturesque**. A work that was sublime was vast and obscure, and had the capacity to inspire terror. In landscape paintings, sharp, craggy cliffs, crashing seas, and swarming skies were considered sublime, whereas calm, harmonious, and familiar settings were deemed picturesque and therefore more Classical. Romantics were attracted to nature, the infinite, and the

ACADEMIES OF ART

During the 18th and 19th centuries, the French and British governments founded a number of royal academies for the instruction of students in the arts. The Royal Academy of Painting and Sculpture in France hosted exhibitions of its members' work. Because they were the only public art shows in Paris, these exhibitions established certain styles, such as Neoclassicism, in favor of others. In England, the Royal Academy of Arts was a private institution free of government direction.

The exhibitions of the British Royal Academy were open to any artist, not just to members. Although the French Royal Academy was dismantled by Napoleon and later revived to merge with other academies, the British Royal Academy today continues to function as it did in the 19th century.

inaccessible ideal. They focused on interior as well as exterior landscapes. As German philosopher Georg Hegel described, "The essence of Romantic art lies in the artistic object's being free, concrete, and the spiritual idea in its very essence—all this revealed to the inner rather than to the outer eye."

At the height of the Romantic era, a powerful emphasis was placed on the study of natural science. Scientists, with new theories of evolution, contemplated the question of how and why humans had come to exist, further underlining the Romantic idea of human beings' importance as individuals. Self-expression and a transfer of emotion from canvas to viewer were essential to Romanticism's individualistic ideas. The ambition of Romantics was to create a work of art that appealed to the senses, emotions, and intelligence of each of its viewers.

Because expressiveness and feeling were applauded, Romantic artists were free to be inspired by a range of subjects, styles, and techniques instead of being constrained by Neoclassical rules. Artists often chose historical or imagined events and striking locations as subject matter. For example, British poet and artist William Blake (1757–1827) painted imaginative scenes from the Bible, including mystical scenes based on the book of Revelation. Fantastical elements such as demons and ghosts were also common. Paintings of the Romantic movement were characterized by strong, vibrant

Francisco de Goya (below) used monsters, demons, and other frightening characters in many of his dreamlike paintings, such as *The Colossus* (c. 1808), to depict forces of fate and nature that are more powerful and devious than humans are often aware.

colors, sharp contrasts of light and dark, and fluid brushstrokes. Although Romantic themes lent themselves best to painting, the style was also prominent in sculpture and architecture. Romantic sculptures often portrayed humans or animals in the midst of action, evoking heightened emotions in their viewers, and Romantic architecture was reminiscent of the Middle Ages with its use of arches and towers.

ROMANTIC ARTISTS

Spanish artist Francisco de Goya (1746–1828) was one of the first to use Romantic ideas in his paintings. He lived during some very troubled times in Spain, including many changes of leadership, a French military occupation, and the appointing of Napoleon's brother as king. Goya's personal life was also fraught with difficulty. Several of his children died in infancy, and in 1792, at the age of 46, he suffered an illness that left him deaf. These experiences played a large role in Goya's work, and many of his images are dark and filled with demons and grotesque monsters, especially his "Black Paintings" (1819–23), which he painted directly on the walls of his house almost exclusively for his own viewing. The "Black Paintings" are darkly colored and portray snarling, evil creatures that devour humans, a reflection of Goya's contemplation of his own internal demons.

Goya had a great influence on later artists, especially French Romantics Théodore Géricault (1791–1824) and Eugène Delacroix (1798–1863). Géricault

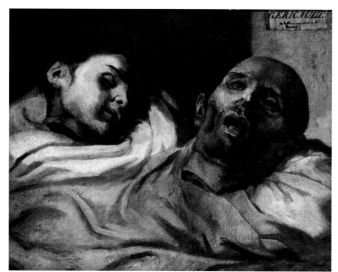

Géricault took his research into the human psyche to an extreme, even studying decapitated heads of torture victims in an attempt to glimpse their mental and emotional states at the time of their death. Such studies were in preparation for his great work, *The Raft of the Medusa* (1819).

had grown up during the years of the French Revolution and the Napoleonic reign and was interested in painting contemporary events, not just to record them but to portray the passion and fire that fueled them. Géricault was also fascinated by the irrationality of the human mind and examined the influence of mental states on the human face. He believed that the face revealed character and set about studying inmates of insane asylums and the severed heads of criminals. His *Portrait of a Child Murderer* (1822) is especially terrifying, for it shows the murderer's suffering as well as her sinister potential.

Géricault died at the young age of 33 after a fall from a horse, but he had already made an impact on the world of Romantic art. His friend, Eugène Delacroix, soaked up Géricault's ideas and became possibly the greatest painter of the Romantic era. After Delacroix was orphaned as a child, he went to live with his uncle, a painter who encouraged the boy's artistic tendencies. Delacroix had Romantic inclinations early on in his work. He often drew from literature, painting works inspired by fictional characters and events. His great work, *The Death of Sardanapalus* (1826–27), was inspired by an 1822 play written by Lord Byron about an ancient king.

Delacroix explored Romantic ideas more fully than any other painter of his time. He worked furiously, expressing his passion with the use of a wide range of colors and the **themes** of liberty, imagination, and the drama and tragedy of life. In 1832, Delacroix traveled to North Africa, an event that affected his art and philosophies for the rest of his life. His imagination was sparked by the sun-soaked landscapes that were so different from those of France. The Arabs of the land had a nobleness that he believed rivaled that of the ancient Greeks and Romans. Even after he returned to France, Delacroix continued to draw from his North African experience, producing another of

Eugène Delacroix's *Dante and Virgil in the Underworld* (1822), based on Dante Alighieri's *Divine Comedy*, portrays the famed Italian poets Dante and Virgil entering the watery underworld. The distinctively tragic and richly colored painting marked Delacroix's landmark debut at the Salon of 1822.

his great paintings, *Women of Algiers in Their Apartment* (1834). His trip to Africa also changed how Delacroix viewed color. True color was rarely seen in nature, he believed. Instead, nature held a never-ending array of **tones**, shades, and reflections. His color theory would influence later artists such as the Impressionists of the late 1800s, who used color and light to translate their perceptions of the world.

While French painters expressed their Romantic tendencies through the figure, German and English artists used the landscape. German artist Caspar David Friedrich (1774–1840) portrayed a spiritual richness in his landscapes. When Friedrich was a child, his mother died from illness, and his brother later died while saving him from drowning. These tragic events led Friedrich to become obsessed with religion and death, themes that occur often in his

From the time John Constable was a young man (below), he had a passion for painting landscapes. While his wife Maria was ill and trying to regain her health at the British seaside resort of Brighton, Constable painted the dramatic *Rainstorm over the Sea* (1824–28).

pieces. He frequently used religious images such as abbeys and graveyards. Even his depiction of trees and the sea, often blanketed with light, snow, or fog, evoked spirituality, as he believed that the artist should paint not only what he saw before him but also what he saw within himself. Early in his career, Friedrich used variations of single colors in his work, and as his career progressed, he continued to limit his color **palette** to two or three hues. His paintings give off an aura of melancholy, divinity, and longing, some of the most prominent Romantic characteristics.

In England, two painters stood at the forefront of Romantic landscape—J. M. W. Turner (1775–1851) and John Constable (1776–1837). Both were landscape artists, and they were nearly the same age, though their careers took different paths. Constable grew up in the English countryside. He loved every tree stump and every pond in this rural area and drew upon it for much of his work, revealing a strong emotional attachment to nature. He was especially interested in light, the sky, and the movement of clouds, producing the largest body of cloud studies in Western art. His paintings capture moments that will soon pass.

After his wife's death in 1828, Constable's work became darker and even more filled with emotion. In 1829, he painted *Hadleigh Castle*, a piece that depicts a castle's ruins after a storm. The forces of nature have had an effect on the castle, weathering it to rubble. Constable didn't receive much recognition for his work until late in life, when Géricault saw his painting *The Hay Wain* (1821) and arranged for it to be exhibited in France.

Constable's friend, J. M. W. Turner, on the other hand, achieved success at a young age and devoted his life almost entirely to making art. He never

Many art historians have found J. M. W. Turner's *The 'Fighting* Téméraire' *Tugged to Her Last Berth to Be Broken Up, 1838* to be symbolic of the changing times Turner witnessed, when old modes of transportation were replaced by steam-powered machines.

married and, with almost no emotional ties to distract him, produced more than 20,000 drawings and paintings in his lifetime. Turner was fascinated by dramatic subjects and often painted the lovely and terrifying aspects of nature, such as crashing waterfalls and the stormy sea. One of his great works, *The 'Fighting* Téméraire' *Tugged to Her Last Berth to Be Broken Up, 1838* (1839), was inspired by a real event in Turner's life. One day while sailing on the Thames River, Turner watched as the once-great battleship, the *Téméraire*, was towed to a wreckage yard. The image stayed with Turner, and he painted the scene using the contrasting themes of life and death and war and peace.

Henry Fuseli (1741–1825) was a Swiss artist who lived in England for most of his career. An early Romantic painter, he set the stage for later artists with his obsession with nightmares and dreams. He painted ghostly apparitions and demons, focusing on the irrational. In *The Nightmare* (1781), a ghoulish creature is sitting upon a sleeping woman's chest. Viewers can almost feel the heavy, pressing weight as they look at the painting.

In the United States, the excitement of discovering and portraying a new and expanding nation fueled Romantic landscape artists. Thomas Cole (1801–48) was born in England and moved to the U.S. when he was 17 years old. He began painting portraits on commission at age 19, but his real love was for landscape. Like his German counterpart Friedrich, he saw God as being present in nature and strove to capture spirituality in his landscapes. He painted grand views of untouched nature, places he recognized as being in danger of urban development.

THE LOUISIANA PURCHASE

In 1803, the U.S. expanded its territory with the Louisiana Purchase. Consisting of more than 530 million acres (214.5 million ha) from the Mississippi River west to the Rocky Mountains, the area had been owned by Spain until Napoleon purchased the land for

France. France officially gained control of the land only a few days before the U.S. bought it. Because much of the Louisiana Territory was yet unexplored, the American wilderness inspired a sense of adventure in the expanding nation's Romantic artists, who rebelled against depicting traditional colonial landscapes.

Every detail in Horace Walpole's home of Strawberry Hill in Twickenham, England, was meticulously redesigned between 1747 and 1792 to reflect the ornate, cathedral-like style of Gothic architecture, from its fireplaces (left) to its façade (opposite).

GREAT WORKS OF THE ROMANTIC ERA

Romantic tendencies in architecture developed in the middle of the 18th century, half a century before the Romantic painting movement took hold. Horace Walpole (1717–97), a British novelist and **amateur** architect, was fascinated by **Gothic** literature and ideas. In 1747, he converted his home, Strawberry Hill, into a sprawling, Gothic castle, complete with turrets, towers, battlements, and corridors. The castle, which took more than 40 years to finish, evoked Romantic fantasies such as damsels in distress and the ghouls and apparitions of the darker side of life. Strawberry Hill inspired other Romantics, such as Constable and Turner, and the Romantic style of architecture became

very popular, especially in Great Britain, with the construction of the Houses of Parliament in London and the renovation of Gothic churches. Gardens were common, and the Romantic characteristic of naturalness—organic lines that blended with the wilderness around them—was soon prized over formal order in architecture and landscaping.

As Romantic architecture sprang up throughout Great Britain, British artists began painting in the Romantic vein. One British masterpiece was George

Walpole, known as the son of England's first prime minister, was also famous as the author of *The Castle of Otranto* (1765), which took its setting from Strawberry Hill and was the first of a flood of Gothic romantic novels made popular in the late 1700s.

Stubbs's (1724–1806) painting *A Lion Attacking a Horse* (1765), a haunting portrayal of nature's wildness and cruelty. In the painting, a horse is desperately trying to dislodge its attacker, a lion, from its back. The dark, rough landscape surrounding the animals adds to the sublime element of the piece. It is said that Stubbs witnessed such an attack on a visit to Morocco, which inspired him to depict the event on canvas. The anatomical details on the horse and lion are so exact that the depiction becomes real and terrifying to the viewer. At the time, the painting raised many philosophical questions about the natural connections between life and death, as well as about the violent side of nature.

One of the best-known and most-copied Romantic paintings is Henry Fuseli's *The Nightmare* (1781). In the painting, a young woman is being tormented by a horrible dream. She has tossed herself partially off her couch and is trapped beneath an incubus, a creature from folklore who was believed to prey upon sleeping women. The incubus, with its large, pointed ears and hairy body, crouches on the woman's chest and seems to be pondering its next move. Behind them, a wild-eyed horse is bursting into the scene. The painting explores the irrational, dark territory of the human subconscious. Fuseli's fascination with dreams is evident in this piece, which served as his personal expression about the feeling of being awakened from a nightmare.

Another Romantic piece that deals with the subconscious is Francisco de Goya's **etching** *The Sleep of Reason Produces Monsters* (1799). In the piece, a man sleeps as winged creatures and a lynx surround him. The etching was an overt attack on Spanish manners and morals. Goya did not believe the Enlightenment theory that rationality and goodness are traits of humanity. Rather, he believed that in the absence of thought, such as in sleep, monsters

Henry Fuseli's *The Nightmare* (opposite) portrayed the contemporary belief that nightmares were the work of demons such as incubi, whose name in Old English was *mare*. The mythological explanation accounted for the oppressive feeling that people experienced after waking from a nightmare.

What the monsters in Goya's *The Sleep of Reason Produces Monsters* etching lack in hostility, those in his "Black Paintings," such as *Saturn Devouring One of His Sons* (above), make up for in disturbing images of nightmarish violence. The 14 scenes Goya painted on the walls of his house were later transferred to canvas to be displayed in museums.

will spring forth. However, the monsters of Goya's piece are not evil, but represent new ideas and inspirations.

In addition to revealing artistic ideas about the subconscious, Romantic art, especially landscape, reflected artists' views on religion. Caspar David Friedrich's landscape *Monk by the Sea* (1810) shows a direct link between spirituality and nature. The figure in the painting, a monk, stands near the turbulent sea. A large expanse of cloudy sky comprises much of the canvas, while the monk is only a minute, almost indiscernible figure. The scale of man to sky is representative of the overwhelming power of the universe and of God himself.

The Raft of the Medusa (1818–19), Théodore Géricault's greatest painting, remains one of the finest masterpieces of the Romantic movement. The painting is based on an event that occurred in 1816, when a French ship, the *Medusa*, wrecked off the west coast of Africa. The ship did not have enough lifeboats for all on board, so the captain ordered his officers to get into the lifeboats. The rest of the crew and passengers were forced to board a raft. Only 15 of the 150 on the raft survived. The French government tried to cover up the incident, but many people found out and were scandalized, blaming the government, which had appointed the elderly and incompetent captain. Géricault gathered as much information about the incident as he could. He interviewed survivors and even took a raft out to sea to study its movements.

The Raft of the Medusa portrays the moment when the castaways try to attract the attention of a passing ship. The survivors and several corpses are piled on top of one another on the floating raft. One man stands on the shoulders of another, waving a piece of cloth toward the sky. Géricault used

When the *Medusa* ran aground, its 6 lifeboats were filled with the 250 most important people, leaving 150 others to fend for themselves. After 15 days, only 15 people remained alive on the raft, as depicted in Géricault's *The Raft of the Medusa*.

Delacroix became France's preeminent Romantic painter in the late 1820s with such melodramatic and voluptuous works as *The Death of Sardanapalus*. Lord Byron's play about the legendary (if not verifiably historical) Assyrian king was written in 1821.

a series of diagonal lines and triangles, all of which build toward the climax of the man signaling the ship. The huge, stormy sea and the helplessness of the men emphasize Géricault's theme of man against nature, a theme that intrigued many painters in the early 19th century. Because the painting was an outright political attack, Géricault changed the title of the piece to *Shipwreck* to keep from attracting government attention. Ironically, after Géricault's death, the French government purchased the piece.

The epic nature of *The Raft of the Medusa* largely influenced Eugène Delacroix's painting *The Death of Sardanapalus*. Delacroix was also inspired by Lord Byron's play about Sardanapalus, a seventh-century B.C. king who sacrificed himself for his land. Delacroix chose to depict the death scene in which all of the king's possessions are brought to him to be destroyed along with him and his court. Delacroix twists the stoicism of the story, though, and portrays Sardanapalus with a scornful, evil expression as he watches the destruction. Delacroix's lines are swift and energetic, and emotion leaps from the painting. Deep reds, golds, and flesh colors pervade the canvas, and smoke from the battle swirls around Sardanapalus. The lounging Sardanapalus is removed from the action, yet he remains the central focus of the piece, an innovative technique for the time period.

Sculpture during the early 19th century was largely Neoclassical, but some sculptors ventured toward the Romantic. Although French sculptor François Rude (1784–1855) was trained in the Neoclassical style, after the fall of Napoleon in 1815, he expressed Romantic characteristics in his work. *The Departure of the Volunteers of 1792* (1833–36), a sculpture commemorating the volunteer army that stopped a Prussian invasion in 1792, decorates the

François Rude's sculptural group *The Departure of the Volunteers of 1792* (left) decorates one base of the Arc de Triomphe; the other three display *The Triumph of 1810* by Jean-Pierre Cortot, and Antoine Étex's *Resistance* and *Peace*.

base of the Arc de Triomphe, a famous monument in central Paris. In the sculpture, the soldiers are urged on by the Goddess of Liberty, who holds a sword high. The motion of the figures and the surge of activity show a passion and excitement rarely seen before in a sculptural group.

French sculptor Antoine-Louis Barye (1795–1875) also tended toward the Romantic in his sculptures, such as *Jaguar Devouring a Hare* (1852), a sculpture of a jaguar crouched over its freshly caught prey. The cat's muscles, the arc of its spine, and the twitch of its tail illustrate Barye's devotion to accuracy. He spent hours at the Paris zoo, often accompanied by his friend Delacroix, sketching the animals. His true-to-life details reinforce the themes of violence and conflict in nature.

THE DECLINE OF ROMANTICISM

During the late 18th and early 19th centuries, the Industrial Revolution changed the face of society, and therefore, the world of art. By the mid-1800s, new innovations in transportation, such as the locomotive, allowed rural dwellers to travel more rapidly to other towns and cities, and knowledge and new ideas quickly became widespread. European countries such as France and England increased colonization in Africa and India, and explorers and travelers brought back cultural ideas and goods from these faraway places, introducing them into European society.

PLACE TO VISIT: THE ARC DE TRIOMPHE

The Arc de Triomphe monument towers more than 164 feet (50 m) tall and 148 feet (45 m) wide at the western end of the Avenue des Champs-Élysées, a street in Paris famous for its shops, cafés, and cinemas. The arch was commissioned in 1806 by Napoleon Bonaparte to commemorate his victory at Austerlitz (a town in the modern-day Czech Republic) in 1805 against invading Austrian and Russian troops, but it was not completed until 1836. At the base of the monument stands François Rude's Romantic sculpture, *The Departure of the Volunteers of 1792*.

INDUSTRIAL REVOLUTION

The Industrial Revolution was a period of major **economic** and technological innovation that changed cultural and social conditions from the late 18th to the mid-19th centuries. Improvements in machinery led to the development of factories and mills—which produced manufactured goods such as fabric and iron—in Europe and around the world. The work of machines replaced traditional manual labor. Ordinary working people found employment in the new factories, though the hours were long and the pay low. The steam engine, fueled by coal, powered the factories and machines, and improved roads and railways allowed goods to be carried quickly from town to town.

As a result of the Industrial Revolution, machines were employed to do work that had been done by hand for centuries. The mechanization of agriculture brought many farmers to the cities or overseas in search of jobs, and the changes in longstanding lifestyles brought a sense of disorder and discontent to many. Because of rapid population growth and urban expansion, the gap between the rich and poor widened immensely.

Adding to the shift in societal classes was the philosophy of Karl Marx and Friedrich Engels, German philosophers who advocated equality between the classes. In 1848, Marx and Engels published their famous work, *The Communist Manifesto*. Commissioned by the **Communist** League, a growing left-wing political party, the *Manifesto* laid out a plan for the overthrow of the wealthy upper class by the working class, with the eventual goal of bringing about a classless society. Marx and Engels believed that **capitalism** was likely to fall and would be replaced by communism. *The Communist Manifesto* shook the world, and after its publication, communism gained followers throughout Europe, Asia, and the Americas.

As the Industrial Revolution and *The Communist Manifesto* gave the working class a more evident place in society, artistic interest shifted from heroic figures such as Napoleon and Sardanapalus to ordinary men and women. With the revolutions of the past behind them, artists began depicting a new sort of hero—the common man. The plight of the working class and the drudgery of everyday life became the subjects of various works of art across Europe. This new movement was called Realism. Francisco de Goya, primarily a Romantic artist, showed seeds of Realism in his work *The Third of May, 1808* (1814). Another prominent artist, Honoré Daumier (1808–79) of France produced a **lithograph** entitled *Rue Transnonain* in 1834, illustrating the unjustified killings of members of the working class by French police. Artists such as Daumier, Goya, and others became the voices of the people, bringing to light their plights, which until then had gone virtually unnoticed and unrepresented in art.

In April 1834, French workers rioted against harsh working conditions and the government's refusal to grant them the right to unionize. In retaliation, many workers and their families were massacred, an event captured by lithographer Honoré Daumier (pictured) in *Rue Transnonain*.

An important invention in the early 1800s made the shift in focus to the working class even sharper: the camera. For the first time, people could capture a permanent photograph on paper. The rise of photography meant that real events and moments in time could be pictured in a truthful way. The camera did not lie. As a result, there arose an increasing artistic bias toward using fact as subject in place of the fictional heroes and events Romantics portrayed. Realists disapproved of traditional and fictional subjects because they were not of the real and present-day experience. Even so, Romantic subject matter persisted throughout the rise of Realism in the latter half of the 19th century, a period known as Late Romanticism.

The quiet, atmospheric landscapes of the French Barbizon school were among the works of Late Romanticism. The Barbizon school was an informal school of artists, including Théodore Rousseau (1812–67), who gathered near Barbizon, France. These artists reacted against a conventional portrayal of nature and used both Realism and Romanticism in their works, aiming to create landscapes and figures that were true to nature but that also evoked traditional Romantic emotions.

Even as the Late Romantics were developing their theories, however, the Positivist Age dawned in Europe and North America. Positivism held that **sensory** experience was the only object of human knowledge; therefore, abstract ideas should be cast aside, and the only knowledge that should be valued was scientific knowledge. Positive consequences could come from the observation of natural and human realms. Positivism was in essence a return to many ideas of the Enlightenment period. Romanticism, therefore, was

In *Departure from the Forest at Fontainebleau at Sunset* (1850–51), Théodore Rousseau's Romantic view of nature can be observed in the images of the sheltering trees, the pink-hued meadow, and the placid cow. Like other members of the Barbizon school, Rousseau sought solace in nature and typically depicted it as a warm, welcoming place.

widely rejected in Positivist thought. The accurate, ordinary, observable world was favored over the subjectivity and irrationality of Romanticism.

In the U.S., it wasn't new thoughts but war that brought an end to Romantic ideals. With the outbreak of the Civil War in 1861, war became a present reality rather than a historic event. The harshness of battle was brought to the forefront of America's consciousness with artists' depictions and photographs of the battlefields, such as those taken by Mathew Brady (1823–96). Unlike early Romantic depictions of heroes, such as Napoleon, in grand uniforms riding bravely into battle, the Civil War photographs showed the soldiers as hungry, dirty, battered men, dispelling glorified ideas of war in many minds.

Despite the effects of Positivism and war, which brought the Late Romantic movement to an end around 1870, Romanticism has had a lasting influence on the art world. The Symbolist movement of the late 19th century was a continuation of the mystical tendencies of Romantic art. Symbolists, like Romantics, were interested in spirituality, dreams, and the imagination. The Symbolists' goal was not just to see objects but to see through them to a deeper and more significant reality, often one that lay within the artist himself. Dreams and the subconscious were the paths to a higher truth, Symbolists thought, and mysticism and spirituality should be embraced by all artists. They believed that there is a fundamental mystery to life, and their aim was to preserve this mystery through their art. French artists Gustave Moreau (1826–98) and Odilon Redon (1840–1916) were at the forefront of Symbolism, and their paintings featured Romantic characteristics, such as exotic settings and supernatural beings.

Photographs such as Alexander Gardner's *Meadow Strewn with Confederate Dead* (1863) grimly portrayed the conflict that pitted North against South. Hired by Mathew Brady as a portrait photographer in 1856, Gardner first worked with

Brady to photograph the war but left to open his own gallery in 1863 after Brady refused to give him proper credit for his work.

Odilon Redon's ghostlike figures and shadowy scenes in works such as *The Walker, Study for 'The Walking Buddha'* (1890–95) reflect the importance of mysticism to the French Symbolists, who believed that a person's subconscious experiences could be expressed through creating art that was subtly abstract rather than an exact copy of life.

The Surrealist movement, begun in 1924 and continuing through the 1930s, was also closely linked to Romanticism. Like Romantic artists, Surrealist artists used elements of fantasy and magic as well as the human subconscious in their work. Expression of true thought, free from reason or moral purpose and unhindered by the artist's consciousness, was the Surrealists' aim. Though transferring subconscious dreams to the canvas without conscious awareness was an impossible task, Surrealists did achieve many dreamlike qualities in their works, as is evident in Spanish artist Salvador Dali's (1904–89) *The Persistence of Memory* (1931), in which objects, such as clocks and tables, have been distorted, as in a dream. Surrealist art often portrayed real, physical objects transformed by the unreality of the dream world, and in this way, Surrealists succeeded in melding Romantic imagination with 20th-century technique.

Even today, much of modern and contemporary art is derived from Romanticism. The Romantics believed in freedom of subject matter and the expression of the individual's internal thoughts and emotions, ideas that have prevailed in art since Romanticism began. Many artists and critics since the Romantic era have held to the idea that self-expression is an important and essential aspect of art and that without it, a piece may lack meaning and intensity. With such ideas, Romantics developed new traditions from the old. From the time of its inception and throughout its rise, Romanticism challenged traditional principles of art and allowed such challenges to recur in the centuries to follow.

PLACE TO VISIT: THE LOUVRE

The Louvre Museum in Paris houses a large collection of Romantic art, including Eugène Delacroix's *The Death of Sardanapalus*, Théodore Géricault's *The Raft of the Medusa*, and Caspar David Friedrich's *Tree of Crows* (1822). The Louvre was previously a palace of French royalty and is now one of the oldest—and most famous—art museums in the world. Visitors can spend hours wandering the corridors and viewing more than 35,000 works of art. Besides Romantic art, the Louvre displays great works of the Renaissance, including Leonardo da Vinci's (1452–1519) *Mona Lisa* (c. 1505), as well as Egyptian art and Islamic art.

TIMELINE

1776	The American colonies announce their independence from Great Britain
1781	Henry Fuseli paints *The Nightmare*
1789	The French Revolution begins six years after the American Revolution's end
1793	In France, King Louis XVI and Queen Marie-Antoinette are executed
1794	Philosopher Thomas Paine writes *The Age of Reason*
1796	Francisco de Goya completes his collection of etchings entitled *Los Caprichos*, which includes *The Sleep of Reason Produces Monsters*
1799	Napoleon overthrows the French government and appoints himself First Consul, and later emperor, ending the French Revolution
1804	Antoine-Jean Gros paints *Napoleon in the Plague House at Jaffa*
1807	Napoleon's army invades Spain and Portugal
1810	Caspar David Friedrich paints *Monk by the Sea*
1812	Lord Byron begins his great work of Romantic poetry, *Childe Harold's Pilgrimage*
1814	The first steam locomotive is developed
1815	Napoleon is defeated, loses power, and is exiled from France
1819	Théodore Géricault finishes *The Raft of the Medusa*
1824	Géricault dies after being thrown from his horse
1825	The first railroad system is established in England
1826	Eugène Delacroix paints *The Death of Sardanapalus*
1836	François Rude finishes the sculpture *The Departure of the Volunteers of 1792* on the base of the Arc de Triomphe
1839	Louis Daguerre publicizes his method of photography
1848	Karl Marx and Friedrich Engels publish *The Communist Manifesto*

GLOSSARY

amateur	someone who does something for pleasure rather than for a career
capitalism	an economic system in which land, houses, and businesses belong to private individuals rather than the government
commissioned	paid to do work for someone
Communist	someone who believes that a country should be organized so that all land, houses, and businesses belong to the government or the community and profits are shared by all
economic	having to do with the way money, goods, and services affect a society
epic	heroic, impressive, or on a very large scale
etching	a picture or print made from an engraved plate; the engraving is done on metal or glass using a sharp object and acid to cut through the surface

ethics	moral principles of human conduct
formality	dependent on conventional shapes and techniques
Gothic	the style of art or architecture prominent in western Europe between the 12th and 16th centuries; Gothic buildings usually have pointed arches and large areas of stained glass
lithograph	a print made by the process of lithography, in which a sheet of paper is pressed over a flat stone upon which an image is drawn
medieval	having to do with the Middle Ages, a period in Europe between A.D. 500 and 1450
monarchy	the type of government that is ruled by royalty, often a king or queen
palette	the colors or kinds of colors used by a specific artist
philosophers	people who study ideas such as truth, wisdom, the nature of reality, and knowledge
picturesque	ordinary and pleasantly beautiful
sensory	having to do with the five senses: taste, touch, smell, hearing, and sight
subconscious	all mental and emotional activities and processes occurring beyond one's awareness
sublime	in art, inspiring awe, fear, power, excitement, or other emotion
themes	the main subjects or ideas of a piece of art
tones	the variations of an original color by adding black or white

BIBLIOGRAPHY

Brion, Marcel. *Art of the Romantic Era*. New York: Frederick A. Praeger, 1966.

Cole, Bruce, and Adelheid Gealt. *Art of the Western World: From Ancient Greece to Post-Modernism*. New York: Simon & Schuster, 1989.

Gardner, Louise. *Art through the Ages*. Orlando, Fla.: Harcourt Brace, 1991.

Gilbert, Rita, and William McCarter. *Living with Art*. 2nd ed. New York: Alfred A. Knopf, 1985.

Johnson, Lee. *Delacroix*. New York: Norton, 1963.

Prideaux, Tom. *The World of Delacroix: 1798–1863*. New York: Time Life Books, 1975.

Rosenblum, Robert. *Modern Painting and the Northern Romantic Tradition: Friedrich to Rothko*. New York: Harper and Row, 1975.

Vaughan, William. *Romanticism and Art*. London: Thames & Hudson, 2003.

INDEX